DIVINE MOTHER AZNA

Daily Comfort to Transform Your Life!

Rebecca Marina Messenger

Copyright 2022 by Rebecca Marina Messenger

All rights reserved. No part of this publication may be reproduced, distributed, or transmitted in any form or by any means, including photocopying, recording, or other electronic or mechanical methods, without the prior written permission of the publisher, except in the case of brief quotations embodied in critical reviews and certain other noncommercial uses permitted by copyright law.

For permission requests, email the publisher at Rebecca@rebeccamarina.com

ISBN: 978-1-7374211-1-5 Print
ISBN: 978-1-7374211-0-8 Ebook

Book Interior and Design by Amit Dey I amitdey2528@gmail.com

Published by Celebration Healing Publishing

Cover art by Pamela McCabe http://pamela-mccabe.artistwebsites.com/

Free Gift!

Video Program: Become MORE magnetic to receive MORE love into your life!

Rebeccamarina.com/resources

OTHER BOOKS BY REBECCA MARINA MESSENGER:

1. <u>Study Edition: The Emerald Tablets of Thoth The Atlantean</u> - Available from Amazon, Barnes and Noble, and other Fine Bookstores
2. <u>The Secret Key To The Emerald Tablets: Revealed By Thoth The Atlantean With His Divine Counterpart</u> - Available from Amazon
3. <u>The Pleiadian Protocol for Reducing Excess Body Mass in Humans: The Never Before Revealed Secret Science from the Stars</u> - Available on Amazon.com
4. <u>Spiritually Decalcify the Pineal Gland</u> - Available on Amazon.com
5. <u>Cure White Sugar and Chocolate Cravings in One Hour: The Simple Secret You Need for Effortless Automatic Control Over Your Cravings</u> - Available on Amazon.com
6. <u>Book of Comfort 1: How the Earth Began, The Origin of Miracles, and a New Connection with Holy Spirit (Book of Comfort, The Messenger Series)</u> - Available on Amazon.com

WHO IS DIVINE MOTHER AZNA?

According to Sylvia Browne, the renowned medium and psychic, Azna is the name that Mother God is known by on the "Other Side."

Azna is the culmination of all of the names of the Divine Feminine. Whether you call Her Isis, Mother Mary, Quan Yin, Lakshmi, Durga Mata, or any other Name… Azna hears and responds.

Just as there are many names for the Father God, so there are many names for the Mother God. Each name has its own qualities, and all aspects of the Divine Feminine are ready and happy to serve.

PERSONAL MESSAGE FROM MOTHER AZNA TO REBECCA

This book is for ME. My name - AZNA. You will write other books as well, keeping to the same theme - that of the Divine Feminine - Mother Mary, Mary Magdalen, Kali, Durga Mata, Lakshmi, Isis, Quan Yin… and many more. In this book… TEACH - **ME** - for I AM the culmination of ALL of the Divine Feminine.

I am **EVERY** stream of Divine Feminine Power.

When Strength is needed, I bring forth My Durga Mata aspect.
When Fierceness is needed, I bring forth My Kali aspect.

When Tenderness is needed, I bring forth My Mother Mary aspect.

When Sensual Wisdom, Healing and Confidence are needed, I bring forth My Mary Magdalen aspect.

When Peace is needed, I bring forth My Quan Yin aspect.
When Prosperity, Wisdom, and Beauty are needed, I bring forth My Lakshmi aspect.

We are ALIVE with the GLORY of ALL that is feminine - whether it be the Divine Feminine - or the feminine aspects within yourself. Both males and females alike, do well to call upon Me and My host of Divine Feminine Aspects.

All that the Divine Feminine and the feminine represent - are a great blessing to every person. Calling upon Me - and recognizing the need for nurturing/nourishing - does NOT diminish in any way, a man's effort to be manly! Indeed, it gives greater depth to his entire being!

A woman calling upon My assistance, would certainly NOT be a wishy-washy, fragile woman! She would not be overly emotional or any of those old, weak attributes, which society has assigned to women. Instead, she would be powerful, strong and more focused than ever!

Now is the time for balancing the male/female ratio in all of humanity - just as in the "Hundredth Monkey Effect." *

It only takes a few strategically placed souls - to vibrate balance and harmony throughout the world.

* Hundredth Monkey Effect - Reference https://www.hundredthmonkey.org/100th-monkey-effect/

The Hundredth Monkey Effect is the spontaneous transference of knowledge throughout a species, once a certain number of individuals has learned a new idea or action. It bypasses physical barriers. It is a mind-to-mind jump… a leap in consciousness.

This idea came from Dr. Watson, who wrote about studies of Japanese monkeys in his book, "Lifetide" (1979). Later, it was used as a parable in Ken Keyes Jr.'s book, "Hundredth Monkey."

Japanese scientists observed the macaca fuscata or Japanese macaque (snow monkey), over a span of 30 years. In 1952, a young monkey, called Imo, solved the problem of dirty raw potatoes. She washed her potatoes in a nearby stream. This new trick was passed along to her mother and playmates, and then to their mothers, and so on... until most of the troop had learned to do the same.

Ultimately, members of these monkey troops on other islands, also exhibited the same behavior.

ABOUT THIS BOOK

This book recounts a series of conversations which I, Rebecca, experienced, as the result of a life-changing encounter with Divine Mother Azna.

Mother Azna wants YOU to know that it is possible for everyone to have conversations with Her… and to receive Her guidance - personally.

(Don't worry! In this book, I give easy instructions on EXACTLY how you can do the same for yourself.)

HOW TO USE THIS BOOK

This book can be read from front to back, back to front, or by opening to any place in between.

When you desire guidance, say a prayer to Mother Azna, then open to any page - and you will find the Wisdom and comfort which you seek.

There are instructions to help you make contact with Mother Azna, at the beginning of this book. The method described, has successfully been used by thousands of my students to communicate directly with the Divine for many years.

SUGGESTED PRAYER -

(or use your own) -

Dear Mother Azna:

Here I am, Your child, in need of Your guidance. Please direct me to the highest path, for the solutions that are best for me now. Thank you for always looking out for me, loving me, and believing in me. Thank you. Amen.

DEDICATION

This book is dedicated to my daughter, Belin, who gave me solace - and a respite from responsibilities - so that I would have the space and time to write this book.

IN GRATITUDE

I am grateful to Lee Ke'aloha Wolf, the most wonderful, thorough editor ever! Your talent, patience and skills are greatly appreciated. Your "Eagle Eyes" constantly amaze me!

IN LOVING MEMORY

Sylvia Browne was a renowned Author, Healer, and Medium. She taught the world about Mother God, Azna.

TABLE OF CONTENTS

Chapter 1: How This Book Came to Be
            (A Life-Transforming Dream) 1

Chapter 2: Instructions For How to Channel Personal
            Guidance From Mother Azna Using Dominant/
            Non-dominant Handwriting Method 14

Chapter 3: Love is the Root of Everything. 28

Chapter 4: Romantic Love - When is it Time to Let Go . . 34

Chapter 5: More on Love. 40

Chapter 6: How to Attract Love or Create MORE Love . . 46

Chapter 7: Attracting Love When You've Been Hurt 50

Chapter 8: What Happens When Love Ain't Working . . . 56

Chapter 9: Forgiveness - When it Hurts 62

Chapter 10: How to Have a Dialogue/Relationship
            With Mother Azna 70

Chapter 11: How to Move Forward 76

Chapter 12: Prayer to Mother Azna for Help 82

Chapter 13: Quiet Minds Find Solutions 84

Chapter 14: People Will Always Find Mother Azna
When the Time is Perfect. 88

Chapter 15: From Chaos to Bliss 92

Chapter 16: Beings of Light - Embrace Your Divinity. 96

Chapter 17: Following Your Heart to Success. 100

Chapter 18: Mother Azna Helps Us to Let Go 104

Chapter 19: Calm Allows Us to Receive 108

Chapter 20: You Must Take Care of Your Own Needs
First - Before Those of Others 112

Chapter 21: Prayer to Recognize Your Gifts 116

Chapter 22: Connectedness Overcomes Loneliness . . . 118

Chapter 23: More Ways to Heal Loneliness 122

Chapter 24: Mother Azna on Exhaustion. 126

Chapter 25: Mother Azna on the Third Eye/Pineal Gland. . 130

Chapter 26: Gratitude is the Attitude 134

Chapter 27: Be Still and Know. 138

Chapter 28: The Divine Energy "Lottery" 142

Chapter 29: Mother Azna on the Universal Law of
Reciprocity 146

Chapter 30: Energy Exercise to Activate Your Third Eye . . 154

Chapter 31: Mother Azna on the 2020 Winter
Solstice/Astrological Great Conjunction. . . . 158

Chapter 32: Final Words of Encouragement. 164

QUOTE:

You may say I'm a dreamer,
but I'm not the only one.
I hope someday you'll join us.
And the world will live as one.

— John Lennon

Chapter One

HOW THIS BOOK CAME TO BE
(A LIFE-TRANSFORMING DREAM)

The idea for this book was conceived during a class that I had taken with a wonderful Spiritual teacher… Debra Ponneman.

Her four-week online class, called "Yes to Success," included many meditations.

During one of the exercises, I had a profound experience!

Debra called this particular exercise, which involved going deeply within - "Meditation for Your Future."

As soon as I entered the trance state, I began to cry. It was as if I KNEW that **something profound is happening now.** The sacredness of the moment caused hot, salty tears to spill unashamedly down my cheeks!

As Debra began to guide the meditation, a REAL-TIME VISION of Divine Mother Azna appeared to me!

Divine Mother was enormous in size - at least ten feet tall - wearing silky robes of soft pink and blue.

She spoke only two words… "TEACH - ME," meaning that She wanted me to teach people about Her. This was made crystal clear to me immediately.

I have loved the Divine Mother for years. I have taught about Her... yet I sensed that She had something deeper for me to do.

I knew that something really big had shifted. Trusting that all would be revealed, I went to bed.

Towards morning, I had a profound dream. This dream experience was SO REAL, that I felt I was REALLY THERE!

In this dream, I was pregnant, and knew that I was in great danger. The sounds of explosions, gunfire and terrified screaming… indicated that I was in a war zone! I desperately needed to hide in order to safely give birth.

There was another pregnant woman with me. She went into labor first. I was able to assist in the birth of her beautiful baby girl, an innocent child born to survive, in spite of the chaos.

We were both terrified for our lives - although the reason for the danger could not be seen - until later when the dream continued.

Then - the dream scene shifted.

There was clearly a war happening… The time was about a hundred years ago. Soldiers stomped through the streets of the village, instilling fear in the terrified residents.

Suddenly, I found myself in a large, old-fashioned hospital ward room.

There were many women lined up on hospital beds, who had all just had babies. As far as the eye could see - ahead and behind - the mothers lay exhausted from giving birth.

The babies, still wet from the birth experience, were lying tenderly on their mothers' chests.

Abruptly… men in uniform burst in!

There were older officers, in charge of younger, conscripted soldiers.

Those who had been conscripted into service were young men, mere boys - 12, 13, 14 years old - **forced to serve!**

An officer was standing over one of the hospital beds, where a woman had just given birth.

The woman's husband was there, as well as three more of her young children.

Many soldiers were gathered around, while the officer was ordering a young conscripted boy to shoot the mother underneath her chin, in order to kill her instantly.

The young boy was crying, the gun shaking in his hand, and pleading... "No, please don't make me do this!"

The mother looked at him with kind eyes. She felt his pain, and his terror.

In mercy, she even raised her chin a little, to make it easier for him to shoot her.

Still - he could not pull the trigger.

The harsh officer became even more demanding and shouted, "Kill her!" A young comrade behind the boy shrieked, "Shoot Church!"

I took this to mean that he should "pretend that the young mother was something that he did not like."

(Perhaps he did not like going to church, or anything that was represented by that.) The young boy, tears streaming down his soot-streaked face, squeezed his eyes shut... and pulled the trigger.

There was blood everywhere!

Noone came to her aid, not even her husband - NOONE!

Standing around the bed were her other young children, watching in horror as their mother was killed before their eyes.

Not one person moved to help her!

I supposed that her husband thought he had better not interfere, or get himself killed, so that he could survive to care for his other children.

The orders from the officers were to go from bed to bed - killing every single one of those new mothers.

Even in the dreamstate, I was absolutely horrified!

I could feel the agony of all of the young soldiers, especially of the juvenile soldier who had pulled the trigger.

I could feel the terror of the other young mothers as they awaited their turn to be killed. Curiously, the soldiers were not killing the babies.

The authorities took some terrible, perverse satisfaction in leaving the babies to be abandoned.

If the babies "made it" long enough… they would be controlled and manipulated into hatred by the twisted government.

The dream continued…

I could feel the abandonment energies of the newborn babies, born amidst this terrible tragedy.

The paralyzing fear of the father and his other young children, who had been forced to witness all of this, hung in the air like a dark cloud of despair.

I felt the father's utter helplessness, as he was forced to choose between defending his wife, yet desperately needing to stay alive in order to care for the children who were left.

Suddenly - I woke up - shaking - yet still in a trance-like state... still experiencing the dream.

Though it was morning, the veil of the dream was still over me. The dream-state persisted.

I went into my morning meditation - unable to shake any of the deep feelings that I was still experiencing.

There were thousands of questions racing through my mind!

I know that this dream was given to me for a reason.

What was the deeper meaning of this dream?

Who were these military men?

Why were these older soldiers forcing the young ones to kill women who had just given birth?

Why would they be ordered to kill helpless, exhausted women, who had just given ALL of their strength in childbirth?

Why did no one come to their aid?

What did "Shoot Church" mean?

Why would the older soldiers force the younger ones to kill the women?

Why didn't they just kill the women themselves?

Even awake, I could still see and feel the emotions of that terrified young boy - the poor little conscripted soldier - who could not have been more than 14 years old.

Tears still streaming down his sooty face, the gun was huge in his hand. If the dream had continued... I feel sure that the boy would have turned the gun on himself.

At that point... I heard the words of the Divine Mother echoing in my head:

This is how they (the Patriarchy) have murdered Me... They have made Me only acceptable as a Virgin in the Church.

The Church preferred to hide My true personality of Power!

Hiding behind outdated laws and precepts - these officers felt that they were righteous in upholding the Patriarchy! They felt that they had the authority to force the young boys into the service of erroneous beliefs.

These evil men felt no remorse over leaving newly-born humans to strive and struggle, without the support of a Loving Mother.

In the same way, purely Patriarchal rule has left all of humanity without the comfort of Divine Mother Love!

Mother Azna continued:

Killing Me won't stop the tide.

The switch to the Divine Feminine Principle is inevitable.

While still in my meditative state, I asked, "Why am I having this dream?" No answer came… until a bit later.

Even after I had left my meditation, and went out to walk my dog, I was still reeling from the dream. I could not shake it. I was sensing all of the terror… as if it were happening to me at that moment. Everything around me felt surreal!

It was as if I were still dreaming… while wide awake!

As soon as I returned from walking my little rescue dog, Tobias, I went right back into meditation.

Then, Wisdom seemed to pour in: Every time you are in blind obedience to the Patriarchal rule, you are supporting those who would kill the Mother.

How and why are young children being forced into the killing of the Mother?

The young mothers could not even protest! They had just given birth, and had no strength left!

These young mothers HAD GIVEN ALL THAT THEY HAD.

In real life this happens to them!

So, in my meditation, I turned to Divine Mother again, and said… "Show me what message You have for me about the dream. I don't believe that it is mere coincidence that You appeared to me last night, and then I experienced this dream the very same night."

It was then that the phrase, "Stop the slaughter of the Mother Principle," started chiming incessantly inside my head.

Still in meditation, I felt guided to sing a song honoring Divine Mother, that I had written a few years ago. (See Rebeccamarina.com/resources)

As I began to sing, Divine Mother appeared to me… yes, twice in 24 hours!

Suddenly, I was back in the dream - only this time - while wide awake in my living room.

Now, Divine Mother was fully present with me.

The dream - the hospital scene, the horror - seemed to be happening in front of me, right in my living room.

Suddenly - a hush fell over the entire assembly - as the Divine Mother arrived in ALL of Her Power and ALL of Her Glory.

The scene froze!

Divine Mother's eyes took in the scene with Great Mercy and Compassion.

The Light of Her heart and gaze transformed ALL of the evil energies in the entire room - into complete Peace and Love.

The room became filled with Her assembly of Angels - known as the Thrones of Divine Mother Azna.

Time stood still!

She touched the gun still being held by the distraught young soldier, tears streaming down his soot-covered face. The gun simply disappeared.

Mother Azna touched the young mother who had just been shot and killed. Instantly, she returned to life - well and whole.

The Divine Mother's personal Angelic Army (the Thrones) then surrounded every bed, every mother, every child, and even every soldier.

The evil energy vanished instantly from every soldier! The conscripted boys were released from the bondage of blind obedience.

All was restored to vibrant, healthy Life!

Divine Mother then turned to me and said... **"When the world calls My Name, the world shall be saved."**

She did NOT mean to call out to Mother Azna specifically... rather She meant to call upon the Divine Mother Principle.

It's important to note that the compassionate Divine Mother did not destroy any of the evil soldiers.

She simply transformed their energies of violence... and neutralized ALL of the hatred from their hearts.

I also noted that Azna showed mercy to the innocent, conscripted soldier, who had been forced to kill the young mother, as Her first "Act of Grace."

Sitting there, with tears streaming down my face, I asked: Mother... What shall I do about this experience?

She replied: **For now Rebecca - just tell the story.**

I felt an immediate release from the horror of the first dream.

Adding negative energy to destruction does nothing to stop/end it. Instead, it can be completely transformed by the Power of Divine Mother Love.

QUOTE:

When many voices are speaking at once, listen to the one most quiet and gentle. That's the one worth listening to.

— **Miranda Linda Weisz**

Chapter Two

INSTRUCTIONS FOR HOW TO CHANNEL PERSONAL GUIDANCE FROM MOTHER AZNA USING DOMINANT/NON-DOMINANT HANDWRITING METHOD

Here are the Basic Instructions for Channeling ANY Being of Light... using the dominant/non-dominant handwriting method.

Your dominant hand is the one which you use most often. It is usually the hand with which you eat and sign important documents. Your non-dominant hand is the one that you use less often.

The majority of people are right-hand dominant. Ten to fifteen percent of the world population are left-hand dominant.

However, even if you are ambidextrous (able to use both hands equally), you still usually favor one hand over the other.

In this book, we are channeling guidance from Mother Azna.

It is easy and natural to Channel, if you allow yourself to relax, and resist being too concerned about getting it perfect.

I have taught hundreds of people to Channel. They were all pleasantly surprised at how easy it was from the very beginning.

It's important to allow yourself to take baby steps. Even the most famous Channel of this century, Esther Hicks (who Channels the group of Spirit Teachers known as Abraham), began very simply.

Esther states that in the very beginning, she wrote words in the air with her nose. She did not become discouraged and kept at the practice.

Now, Esther has Channeled the group of Spirit Teachers known as Abraham, for thousands of people around the world.

Beings of Light use Channeling to transmit Wisdom from Heavenly Realms into the third dimension.

Beings of Light are very eager to transmit their Wisdom, Love and Support. Yet, they need a human to be the voice. Let us begin by helping you to find - and use - your own beautiful voice.

It's important to establish WHY you desire to Channel, whether it is Mother Azna, or ANY Being of Light!

Are you seeking specific information for your own personal guidance?

Are you seeking to transmit messages for the benefit of others?

Are you seeking to do this just for fun?

All reasons are valid, good, and no cause for shame or embarrassment.

Would you like to know what every Light Being, including Mother Azna, **wants from you?**

First and foremost, Light Beings want a **relationship with you**, **more** than they want anything else. This is why I recommend that you begin to Channel by establishing a relationship with the Light Being that is Mother Azna.

After all, would you like it if someone just wanted to ask you all kinds of questions, without even getting to know you? That would be very disrespectful.

So always begin by establishing a relationship with any Being of Light whom you wish to Channel.

For Mother Azna... I suggest that you write a greeting to Mother Azna, with your dominant hand, which could possibly say… Dear Mother Azna: I desire to form a relationship with you. Is that okay?

Now, SWITCH the pen into your non-dominant hand. Be still for a moment. You will probably just get **one or two words** in response - or maybe more - as all Spiritual information comes through the right side of the brain.

Your non-dominant hand is HARDWIRED to the right side of your brain. **Being either right or left-handed does NOT affect this phenomenon.** Spiritual Information will ALWAYS come through the right side of your brain first.

It's very important that you actually WRITE out the question, because there is MAGIC in the switching. When you write a question with your dominant hand, and then SWITCH to your non-dominant hand to write your response, **something special happens within your brain.**

You are actually creating **New Neural Pathways** between the right hemisphere of the brain and the left hemisphere of the brain. Information is transmitted via the Corpus Callosum, which is the thick bundle of nerves separating and connecting the right and left hemispheres of the brain.

Each time you do this exercise, you are creating more Neural Pathways. Soon, what seemed like a dim, narrow path, will become a bright super-highway! With practice, you are able to receive Channeled information easily.

The great Light Being, Sanat Kumara, told me in a Channeling session, that the Corpus Callosum is a marvelous map system! This sensitive bundle of nerves already contains a pathway for every Being of Light whom you may ever desire to Channel.

As you continue to do this exercise... writing a question with the dominant hand, then switching the pen to answer with the non-dominant hand... you create **many** new Neural Pathways. Then information begins to flow very easily and rapidly for you.

I have been Channeling for many years, and yet, whenever I meet a new Being of Light, who desires for me to Channel information for them... I always take a few days to do dominant/non-dominant handwriting with them.

This increases the ease of communication exponentially!

It's important to start out with baby step questions.

As I said earlier, establishing a relationship is KEY.

Below are some questions which I suggest that you use to start. Remember, it's very important to WRITE out the question... even though I've written it for you... and **then** SWITCH to the non-dominant hand to receive the answer.

As always, Spiritual information will come through the right side of your brain. You **will not be possessed by some Spirit** who comes in to move your hand!

There is a field of study in which it does happen - that a Spirit will cause your hand to move. It is called "automatic writing." **This is NOT that study**.

You are NOT possessed... however, the information does flow into the right side of your brain... perhaps one tiny word at a time.

It's important to be gentle with yourself. Resist being impatient. Just take this one baby step at a time.

Also, be cautious of the questions which you decide to ask.

DO NOT be asking "fortune-telling" questions...

How do I know what constitutes a "fortune-telling" question?

Anything that demands that Mother Azna foretell the future is considered a "fortune-telling" question. Not even God has dominion over the FREE WILL of mankind.

There are always humans involved in every decision... and every single human has their own FREE WILL. Therefore, it is impossible for any being to accurately predict the future every time. **IT IS POSSIBLE** to make a prediction "based on the energy as it appears now."

Examples of "fortune-telling" questions are:

- **When will my true love come**? He or she has FREE WILL... and you CANNOT impose your will on theirs...
- **When will this situation be resolved?** Again, other people and their FREE WILL are involved.
- If I play these numbers in the lottery... will I win?

    OH, PLEASE! If you want to Channel ONLY for "fortune-telling" reasons, you will BLOCK the flow of guidance from Mother Azna!

Better questions are: HOW can I accomplish something or... WHAT action can I take toward my goal?

Example:

- HOW can I get ready to attract my true love?
- WHAT can I DO to resolve this situation?
- WHAT can I DO to "win big" in life?

Do you see the difference in these questions?

Remember that Mother Azna is looking for a relationship and a partnership. When you ask HOW or WHAT... you are taking responsibility for **your part.**

Know that Mother Azna (or ANY Light Being) desires to be of service to humanity... not your puppet! Also, remember what I said earlier, about being a friend and establishing a relationship. You would not be happy if someone only liked you because of the information that you could give them, would you? Keep that in mind as you begin this exercise...

Now you are ready to begin...

Put your pen into your dominant hand and write out one of these questions.

It is IMPORTANT to WRITE the question with your dominant hand (even though I just wrote it FOR you). There is MAGIC in the actual SWITCHING of your hands! **Don't cheat yourself of this MAGIC.**

With your dominant hand, WRITE… **Dear Mother Azna: I would like to establish a relationship with You. Is there anything that You would like to say to me now?**

WRITE the above question here: _____

_____

_____

_____

Now, SWITCH the pen into your non-dominant hand, and allow information to flow to you… one word at a time. Remember that no Spirit is going to come to move your hand! The Wisdom is coming from Mother Azna… through the right side of your brain.

Write the response here… Give yourself plenty of room... as you will write big and sloppy. (Notice that the spacing is extra roomy.)

Write Mother Azna's response here:

_____

_____

_____

After you have done that part of the exercise... move to another question. Put your pen back into your dominant hand, and write this... **Dear Mother Azna: Is there anything that I can do for You?**

WRITE the above question here: _____

_____

_____

_____

Now, SWITCH the pen back into your non-dominant hand. Allow the Wisdom to flow... one little word at a time.

WRITE Mother Azna's response here:

_____

_____

_____

_____

I suggest that you repeat these two questions daily, until you begin to feel that the information is flowing more easily.

Expect that you're going to write big and sloppy, with the non-dominant hand. **That is perfectly right and good.**

It's important NOT to criticize yourself. And it's important NOT to be concerned that "nobody could read this." Nobody else is **supposed** to read this... except for YOU. This is your exercise, for your own Spiritual growth.

This is JUST THE BEGINNING of your relationship with Mother Azna. It is up to you to continue, and formulate more questions until the information flows more smoothly. As you progress, you may find that you do not need to ask questions at all. Just sit with pen in hand... and invite Mother Azna to come to you.

You may desire to ask for more guidance on what you have received. Simply repeat the handwriting process asking:

- Will You please give me more clarity on what You said?
- What can I do to communicate with You more effectively?
- Do You see any Spiritual or mental blocks? If You do, please let me know what they are, and what I can do to release/heal them.

I would love to hear some of your experiences with this… so please drop me a line to tell me how you're doing: Rebecca@Rebeccamarina.com

There will be space for you to use to write at the end of some chapters. You may desire to have more guidance from Mother Azna on that chapter's topic. As you become accustomed to receiving Channeled guidance, you will begin to formulate your own questions.

My very favorite question to ask of ANY Being of Light is this: Dear _____: What shall we create together today? This opens the door for unlimited Creativity and Inspiration!

WRITE the above question here: _____

_____

_____

_____

_____

_____

_____

Now, SWITCH the pen back into your non-dominant hand. Allow the Wisdom to flow... one little word at a time. WRITE the Light Being's response here:

_____

_____

_____

_____

_____

_____

QUOTE:

For one who knows Me, I am one with him;
for one who wants to know Me,
I am very near to him;
and for one who does not know Me,
I am a beggar before him.

— Anandamayi Ma

Chapter Three

LOVE IS THE ROOT OF EVERYTHING

Rebecca: Dear Divine Mother: What is the ONE thing which You would most love to help people to understand - that will improve their lives the most?

Mother Azna responds: I would help them to understand that LOVE really is the ROOT of EVERYTHING!

Even when people seem to do evil things, it is often due to some kind of **mis-guided effort to Love.**

How can this be so? I ask.

Mother Azna replies: When a person steals, it is usually because they have LOVE for sustenance, and sometimes because they have LOVE for survival!

When one country wages war on another, it is because those in power love THEIR country. They feel that they are right to take from another, in order to improve their own country.

If you keep looking at any situation, digging deep, you will find some type of quest for Love at the heart of it.

Of course, there is healthy Love… and there is misguided/unhealthy Love.

When Love is paired with fear of any kind, it can be detrimental.

One example could be… When a mother prays for her son to stop drinking (or anything that she feels is not good for him), it is because she LOVES him and fears for his safety.

The mother only knows her own Love and fear. She cannot know the SOUL PLAN of her child. Perhaps that child needs to sink down even lower, in order to learn his/her own lesson *that will stick with him/her for life.*

Many pioneers of change in substance abuse were at their very lowest level possible. It was in this rock-bottom state that inspiration for change was born.

Let's go back to the discussion of war. While it is true that one country may feel Love for their own and seek to expand by taking from another - there is both Love and fear at work here.

In your own lives, seek to have that pure Love that is not tainted by fear.

For most cases it is the "fear of loss" that inhibits a solid Love relationship of any type.

You can ask for help from your own Inner Being/Inner Wisdom, to be more in the state of pure Love.

Perfect Love Casts Out Fear from the Christian Scripture:

> There is no fear in Love, but perfect Love casts out fear. For fear has to do with punishment, and whoever fears - has not been perfected in Love.
>
> 1 John 4:18

You are already on your way to experiencing and expressing perfect Love!

Optional Exercise: (Use the instructions at the beginning of this book on Channeling guidance from Mother Azna.)

WRITE with your dominant hand: Dear Mother Azna: How can I show more Love and Mercy to myself?

Please WRITE out the question. There is MAGIC when you SWITCH to the non-dominant hand to write the response. There is space to write the question below - or use a separate sheet if you desire.

_____

_____

_____

_____

_____

_____

_____

_____

_____

Now, SWITCH the pen to your non-dominant hand. Be patient. Write down the first words that come to you. Let this be easy. Do not stress.
Mother Azna reponds:

_____

_____

_____

_____

_____

_____

QUOTE:

One common mistake is to think that
ONE reality is THE reality.
You must always be prepared to leave
one reality for a greater one.

— **Mother Meera**

Chapter Four

ROMANTIC LOVE - WHEN IS IT TIME TO LET GO?

Let us speak of Love today... Romantic Love!
At first - Love can be fresh, fun, exciting - then later, it can turn sour!

Many times, this difficulty is due to the old "baggage" of one or both parties, who bring old "stuff" into the relationship.

Old emotional wounds - that have not been healed - are extremely detrimental to any relationship.
If this is the case, it is important to go within your heart and recognize what needs healing.

If BOTH parties have a LOT of old, unhealed pain… it is very likely too much of a burden for the relationship to survive.

Sometimes, even in a long-term relationship - there comes a breaking point. Yes, a point where the union is doing more harm than good. You will know if/when this occurs for you.

Now, if the union has been in place for a prolonged period of time, it may be VERY difficult to let it go! You have been programmed - brainwashed - to hold onto a relationship at all costs. Sometimes the relationship has become very toxic, and there is simply no saving it.

One of Rebecca's dear friends always says that sometimes a relationship is simply COMPLETE in the status that it held. This gives a chance for healing, and moving forward into a different kind of relationship.

Rebecca: This is so very true in the case of my relationship with Henry - my former husband of 24 years. Now divorced, our relationship has shifted into a very dear friendship. I would (and have) come to his aid in a crisis. He would (and has) come to my aid in a crisis.

Azna says: Ask for help and guidance in this manner:

Dear Divine: Please open my eyes so that I may see a clear path before me.
If continuing this relationship is for my/our highest good, please make that clear. If this relationship is NOT for my/our highest good, then please make that clear quickly.

And please make it as painless as possible!
Thank you. Amen.

This advice applies to romantic, business, family, and friend relationships as well.

Sometimes… there is something wonderful waiting, just on the other side of letting go.

Be advised - as long as you are in any kind of blame, or victim energy, you are NOT ready for a new situation.

If you try a new relationship before you have healed the old one - you WILL bring old, unpleasant baggage with you.

Rebecca: USE CAUTION: The above prayer is very powerful! Once, I said this prayer about a man whom I was dating. He lived in another state and would fly into my city - a couple of times a month - just to be with me.

The very next day - AFTER I said this prayer about him - he surprised me by flying in to take me out to a fancy dinner. You guessed it! He did it, just so that he could break up with me in a public place - hoping that I would not make a scene!

Looking back, it would have been DISASTROUS for our relationship to continue.

Optional Exercise: (Use the instructions at the beginning of this book on Channeling guidance from Mother Azna.)

WRITE with your dominant hand: Dear Mother Azna: Will you please help me to know for sure when it is time to let go - or show me how I can make this relationship better?

Please WRITE the question with your dominant hand. There is MAGIC when you SWITCH to the non-dominant hand for the response. Space to write the question below - or use a separate sheet.

_____

_____

_____

_____

_____

_____

_____

Now, SWITCH the pen to your non-dominant hand. Be patient. Write down the first words that come to you. Let this be easy. Do not stress.
Mother Azna reponds:

_____

_____

_____

_____

_____

_____

_____

QUOTE:

To love is to recognize yourself in another.

— Eckhart Tolle

Chapter Five

MORE ON LOVE

Much Love is in the air, or atmosphere, for all of humanity. All that is needed... is to be still and **request an upgrade** of Loving feelings.

You may think this sounds far too simple - until you **experience** the following exercise.

Notice that I did not say - until you "try" this, as using the word "try" can set one up for failure. Instead, I used the phrase... until you EXPERIENCE this.

Exercise:
Sit quietly. Touch your tongue briefly to the roof of your mouth, and say... "I desire to receive more Love energy."
Notice that you begin to feel more peaceful.

(Touching the tongue to the roof of the mouth is an ancient yogi secret called "The Bagha." This tells the brain: Pay attention! Something important is happening!)

It is in the sharing… that Love grows.
Yes, you receive Love for yourself. Yet, just as money invested will grow and increase - so Love energy does likewise.

The Bank of Love energy will NEVER RUN OUT.

You may withdraw from the bank at will, and you may invest at will. You invest in the Bank of Love by doing Loving actions to/for another.

Sometimes just thinking and sending Loving Thoughts to another is sufficient.

Always remember to do Loving actions for yourself as well!

Be still, and if Spirit brings someone to your heart, pay attention to your guidance.

Is there something that you feel directed to do for that person?
If the one who comes to your mind is hungry, or needy, share sustenance as guided… and only as guided.

You could be the Angel for whom someone has been praying.

If the person who comes to your awareness feels sad, ask for guidance on how to comfort them.
If they are filled with anxiety - ask how best to calm them.

Often, the thing that you are guided to do for someone... will be a big stretch for you.
Rejoice! Stretching helps you to grow!

Mother Azna says: This reminds me of the time that Rebecca was guided to give a sum of money to a woman, to help with a health issue. She had a horrible toothache and needed a root canal, which she was unable to afford. Rebecca heard the woman's soul crying out for help... and responded.

Rebecca resisted a bit at first - having the thought that she didn't have that much money in her checking account. She would have to go into her savings account - the one that had been set aside for a down payment on a house one day.

Still... Rebecca kept getting the same guidance - and decided to TRUST. So, she took that money out of her savings - and presented it to the lady.
Yes, Rebecca decided to trust that if she acted on her guidance - that all would be well.

Then, for the rest of that month - Rebecca was rewarded for taking the guided action - she received ten times more than she had gifted.

Rebecca shares her personal insight on giving:

It is important to note that you don't ever give... just to get a **reward**.

You give a gift... because you are guided from your heart to do so.

The reward can come in many different ways - and in the timing that is for your highest good.

You can never go wrong when you are "in the black" with the Universe!

If all humans were attuned to their inner guidance, and gave as they were prompted, there would be no hunger in the world.

Of course, some people choose a harsh life path in order to work on their Soul growth. Sometimes entire groups of people come in to experience poverty... because of their Soul missions.

Coming into an incarnation with poverty consciousness... is never encouraged by one's team of Spiritual advisors. However, even in Heaven, free will is respected.

Exercise: (Use the instructions at the beginning of this book on channeling guidance from Mother Azna.)

WRITE with your dominant hand: Dear Mother Azna: How can I pay more attention to when it is time to give to others?

Please WRITE the question. There will be MAGIC when you SWITCH to the non-dominant hand to write the answer. Space to write the question below - or use a separate sheet.

_____

_____

Now, SWITCH the pen to your non-dominant hand. Be patient. Write down the first words that come to you. Let this be easy. Do not stress.
Mother Azna reponds:

_____

_____

_____

_____

QUOTE:

Do you want to meet the love of your life?
Look in the mirror.

— Ms. Byron Katie

Chapter Six

HOW TO ATTRACT LOVE OR CREATE MORE LOVE

Rebecca: Dear Azna: Will you please give us some insight as to how to attract a Loving partner, or how to create more Love within the relationships in which we already find ourselves?

Mother Azna replies: Yes, there are many lonely people who are desiring a Loving partner. There is no need for anyone to be lonely. There is already a Loving partner waiting for just the right "attractor beam" to be pointed in their direction.

The moment that you have a longing - the answer to that longing is identified in Spirit. In Truth, there are several suitable matches for every lonely heart out there. There are several actions which one can take, to make potential romantic unions happen faster.

Notice that I said "**Actions**." Here is a list of "Actions" that start the "attractor beams" magnetizing Love to you more quickly:

- **Action Number One**: Get clear on the kind of relationship which you desire. The Universe Loves **clarity**. Without clarity - it's like being at a restaurant and just telling the server, "Please bring me some food - I'm hungry." There is no telling what dish the server might bring to you.

- **Action Number Two**: Get clear on **how** you desire to **feel** in this relationship.

- **Action Number Three**: Get clear on what you are **willing to give** in this relationship.

- **Action Number Four**: Get clear on what you are **NOT willing to give** or endure in this relationship.

- **Action Number Five:** Get clear on what you are **willing to weed out** in your own life to make room for this relationship.

It is far more important to focus on the way that you desire to feel - rather than getting very specific about appearance - height, weight, hair color, etc.

If a person makes you feel a certain delicious way, you will easily forget about how tall or short he/she is.

Rebecca jokingly says that she doesn't care if a man is a hundred pounds overweight, as long as he dances well. That alone can make her feel super-attracted to a man. It is different for everyone. Act as if you are going to meet this person at any and every moment.

Rebecca: Be Prime Real Estate - don't leave the house without looking your best. Be well-groomed at all times.

When you put a piece of Real Estate on the market, you do everything possible to make it Prime Real Estate.

These actions get the attraction flowing. Movement like this quickly gets you closer to where you desire to be.

It is also important to clear out old emotional baggage.

QUOTE:

Love cannot live where there is no trust.

— **Edith Hamilton**

Chapter Seven

ATTRACTING LOVE WHEN YOU'VE BEEN HURT

Rebecca: Dear Mother Azna: I have numerous clients who desire to find romantic Love. However, many of them have been so hurt in the past, that they find it almost impossible to trust another potential partner. Do you have any advice for them?

Mother Azna responds: Being unable to trust is one huge factor that stops the flow of Love. This inability can repel Love and prevent the attraction of a partner to you.

It is vitally important that a person realizes exactly WHAT it is that they are not trusting.

Is it your own self?

Is it another person?

What I see most often... is that a person does not trust him/herself, due to the past mistakes that have been made. They feel as though they simply don't have what it takes, to make sound decisions about Love.

When you combine this "non-trust" of self with "non-trust" of the prospective partner, you can be sure that you will NOT attract a healthy Love life.

Rebecca: So, what is the solution?

Mother Azna replies: The solution is to look within your own heart and find the hidden source of pain. Until you know what the root cause of your deepest pain and mistrust is, you cannot ferret it out.

It is my suggestion to use the healing method which I have given to Rebecca to dig out the seed... and heal it. Rebecca calls the method HPT or Heart Point Technique.

Instructions on using Heart Point Technique follow:

Set the intent that you desire to dig out and transform the source of your deepest pain. Get specific. You are looking for the pain that causes you NOT to trust, either yourself, others, or both.

Place your hands in the HPT position as shown. This connects the heart and the head… especially the emotional centers.

Call in the "Light of Revelation" into the Higher Self Point which is 18-24 inches above the head. The HSP is like a gateway to the Divine. You may call any type of Light into it… and it WILL come!

Still holding the position, call the Light of Revelation in through the crown, and slowly down through the body until it reaches the heart. Your heart holds all of the secrets to your healing!

Begin repeating these words: I do not trust myself. I do not trust others. I have pain that causes me NOT to trust. Divine Mother please show me the solution.

If your hands are tired, take them out of the HPT position. Relax and allow some Revelation to come to you. It may be very subtle.

Then, have a conversation with the PAIN. Dear PAIN: I'm sorry that you have suffered. What kind of energy will make you feel better?

Listen. You will receive some sort of guidance. Then ask: WHO do you trust to GIVE you the energy that will make you feel better? You will get some kind of sensation from your conversation with the PAIN. The Being whom your PAIN trusts can be a Deity Figure, a person, living or dead, or a friend or family member.

Call that Being to you. Ask them to give your PAIN the healing energy that was requested. Thank them... and be willing to receive.

That's the simple version of Heart Point Technique. DO NOT be fooled by the SIMPLICITY. You are on your way to HEALING.

Congratulations! You took some ACTION! More importantly... you took action to work on your own PAIN. In the coming days, take note of how you notice your heart opening to more TRUST!

Without TRUST, there can be no healthy relationship!

QUOTE:

Our attitude towards others determines their attitude towards us.

— Earl Nightingale

Chapter Eight

WHAT HAPPENS WHEN LOVE AIN'T WORKING?

Rebecca: Mother Azna: What if you are already in a relationship that is not very satisfying?

Divine Mother replies: Time again to take some action.

This time the action comes in the form of a decision.

Do I want to keep this relationship and cause it to be revived? Or do I desire to "kick it to the curb," suffer the break-up consequences, and start all over?

Sometimes, it is true that a relationship is simply complete in its current phase. A relationship can be shifted from romance to friendship - if both parties are evolved enough to see the value of friendship. Most times… this is not the case.

Often one or both parties think that the grass is "greener" on the other side of the fence.

Usually the grass on the other side is just DIFFERENT grass - NOT BETTER grass.

To improve the relationship in which you currently find yourself, action must be taken.

It is not beneficial to end a relationship simply because it has gone a bit stale.

Here is how to find out MORE about your current relationship:

Action steps:

- Write down a list of all of the things that attracted you to this person in the first place.
- Let yourself daydream about how wonderful that **felt**. This alone helps to shift your energy. Your partner will feel it too… even if you don't say a word.
- Next, actually say some of these things to your partner - for instance, "When we were first together, I felt so _____, when you _____."

Say this with Love - then, begin to notice all of the things which you appreciate about your partner now. Express these things with sincerity, and in the energy of appreciation!

Mother Azna continues: Once - when Rebecca was having issues in her marriage - she helped to lighten the situation by doing a "card trick." She took regular three-by-five index cards, and cut them in half. Each morning, she wrote something that she appreciated about herself, on one half of the card… then, something she appreciated about her husband, on the other half.

Rebecca then presented his half to her husband.

He loved those cards! He kept them - held firmly in a rubber band - in his truck - for years.

Yes, you may feel that you have to do the bulk of the work in sprucing up a relationship, but you will find that the rewards are very great. Praying and visioning you two together in a happier state, is also very beneficial. **The key here is to take some positive action.**

Optional Exercise: (Use the instructions at the beginning of this book on Channeling guidance from Mother Azna.)

WRITE with your dominant hand: Dear Mother Azna: Do You have any guidance for me about this relationship?

Please WRITE the question as there is MAGIC when you SWITCH to the non-dominant hand.
Space to write the question below - or use a separate sheet.

_____

_____

_____

_____

_____

_____

_____

_____

Now, SWITCH the pen to your non-dominant hand. Be patient. Write down the first words that come to you. Let this be easy. Do not stress.
Mother Azna reponds:

_____

_____

_____

_____

_____

_____

_____

QUOTE:

Not forgiving is like harboring a hidden parasite.
It slowly eats away at your energy,
silently robbing you of your life force,
and your best vitality.

—Rebecca Marina Messenger

Chapter Nine

FORGIVENESS - WHEN IT HURTS

Rebecca: Dear Mother Azna: Thank you for all of the bountiful blessings which you so Lovingly bestow upon me. Today - please show me a way to make peace with a certain person who feels that I have wronged them.

There is a person in my life who bears ill will towards me. This person harbors resentment over something which they feel I did to harm them. It doesn't matter that I HAD NO EVIL intentions. This person PERCEIVES that I did wrong. **Therefore, in their eyes, I did them wrong.** I require assistance to make peace with this person.

Mother Azna replies: One of the greatest accomplishments which you can achieve, is to make peace in your heart - peace with all those who have harmed you or that you have harmed. I suggest that you do this one-person-at-a-time. The benefits to both you - and the other party - are enormous.

Azna continues: You see, ALL SOULS do love each other. If someone has harmed you, be assured that you BOTH planned to experience this situation before this incarnation.
Perhaps you desired to learn about forgiveness. Perhaps they had agreed to volunteer to dampen their Light, and take the role of the "bad guy," in order for YOU to experience deeper levels of forgiveness.

- NOTE: In my opinion… the best book to explain this is "The Little Soul and the Sun" by Neale Donald Walsch

Rebecca: Mother Azna then reminded me of a powerful exercise that I had previously created for some of my clients. (Physician heal thyself!)

FORGIVENESS EXERCISE:

This is how to begin the Forgiveness Exercise:

This is not accomplished with your logical mind. It is both begun and ended with your Spirit mind. This exercise will help you to determine WHO in your life needs forgiveness… or needs to forgive you!

(For a video of this exercise, please visit: rebeccamarina.com/resources)

Your logical mind will go racing to bring up all of the people who have harmed you in some way. Only your heart knows who is the biggest obstacle to your abundant flow.

Use the Heart Point Technique method - (which was described in detail earlier in this book):

Sit quietly. Take some slow, peaceful breaths. Put one hand over your eyes, and one hand over your heart. Ask the Divine Mother energy to pour in through your crown, and trickle down to your heart.

Dear Azna: Please show me who I need to forgive first.

This is your plea. As you do this, a certain person will come to mind.

Who it is… may surprise you. Often, it is not the big happenings in our lives, but the smallest, forgotten ones that are pulling on our energy.

Ask for assistance in forgiving this person. You are not done yet. It is very good, in human reality, to take some physical-action steps. Don't worry that you will have to face them physically.

It is NOT necessary to reach out to them in person... unless you are guided to do so, after you take the action steps listed below:

- Use an index card or a stiff piece of paper - stiff enough so that when held at eye level - it will stay flat and readable.
- Draw a stick figure of the person. This will serve as an avatar to represent the person.
- Hold the card slightly above eye level to activate your emotional centers.

You are putting some physical action into your prayer when you do this.
You may feel a heaviness as you are doing this.

You may feel like saying, "But Mother, that person did **ME** wrong. I feel that I did nothing to them." And Mother Azna would say to you: Do you desire to have freedom from this heaviness, or do you desire to remain stuck forever?

Hold the card up - just above eye level. We suggest saying the Hawaiian Ho'oponopono* Prayer below:

I Love you.
I'm sorry.
Please forgive me.
Thank you.

*Ho'oponopono is a Hawaiian word/conflict resolution exercise - meaning "to put things right."
(Pronounced - ho'-o-po-no-po-no)

Do this daily until you feel no charge of anger or resentment at all when you think of this person/situation.

A faster way to achieve complete forgiveness is to say the prayer - while looking at the avatar you have made (the stick figure), several times daily.

Doing this action means that you are taking the responsibility for the Soul contract that you had made with this person.

When you feel the energy shift, you can say, "This portion of our Soul contract has ended."

You may desire to take a few days to integrate this work before moving on to another person. Sometimes, you have forgiven someone a little, yet not completely, and you have not let it go.

You will be surprised at the amount of energy you will regain after doing this exercise.

Optional Exercise: (Use the instructions at the beginning of this book on Channeling guidance from Mother Azna.)

WRITE with your dominant hand: Dear Mother Azna: Is there anything, or anyone, to whom I need to send more forgiveness?

Please WRITE the question as there is MAGIC when you SWITCH to the non-dominant hand.
Space to write the question below - or use a separate sheet.

_____

_____

_____

_____

_____

_____

_____

Now, SWITCH the pen to your non-dominant hand. Be patient. Write down the first words that come to you. Let this be easy. Do not stress.
Mother Azna reponds:

_____

_____

_____

_____

_____

_____

_____

QUOTE:

Your true character is most accurately measured by how you treat those who can do Nothing for you.

— **Mother Teresa**

Chapter Ten

HOW TO HAVE A DIALOGUE/RELATIONSHIP WITH MOTHER AZNA

Rebecca: Dear Mother Azna: Thank you for always being here for us - even when we ignore Your presence and the Power that You have to help. Please give us a message today... that will uplift even the heaviest of hearts.

Mother Azna replies: Darling children, for I do consider you all to be My children, even though you may resist the idea of a Feminine Deity, there can be no true creation without some female involvement.

When the whole world calls my Name, the whole world shall be saved.

It need not be every single person. Just one voice in a community... is enough to shower the whole community with Divine Mother Blessings. There are many Names attributed to the Divine Mother Energy.

All of these Names are good to use. However, there will be one Name that resonates more in your own heart than another.

Keep in mind that all feminine Deities have their own special talents. Just as Angels have specialties, so does every aspect of the Divine. It is important to approach any Being of Light with a sense of Love. Yes, Love for them, and especially Love for yourself.

If you feel that you are not connected enough to feel real LOVE for a certain Light Being… the next best thing is APPRECIATION!

Just like Real Estate, whatever you appreciate grows in value. Appreciation can cause a relationship to grow faster than trying to force Love. Appreciation always leads to deeper feelings!

As all Divine Beings have said so many times… We desire a relationship, not a beggar's union.

There is NEVER a need to beg any Light Being for favors. Neither can We be bribed.

As you realize the gift that you are to Us - so shall We be blessed.

It is our desire for you to evolve. A sure sign that this is happening for you - is when you come to Us in partnership. Yes, desiring a relationship with Us. I am Mother Azna. I desire a back-and-forth relationship with **you. Yes, you, the person reading this book right now.**

Mother Azna continued: Write to Me. I adore receiving Love letters from my children. As any nurturing mother, of any species, enjoys being appreciated and loved by her offspring - so do I.

Here is the prayer to get you started:

Dear Mother Azna: I may not have known of You until now, yet I desire to begin a relationship with You. Please show me how to have a relationship with You. Thank You. Amen.

Next, be on the lookout for ways that I show you that you are heard and loved.

Perhaps you will find a flower in an unexpected place. You may see bees - or any type of winged creature - suddenly cross your path. Even frogs can be a sign - as frogs show the evolution process so well.

Be especially aware of any new and delicious odors, for I often show My presence using the power of smell.

Optional Exercise: (Use the instructions at the beginning of this book on Channeling guidance from Mother Azna.)

WRITE with your dominant hand: Dear Mother Azna: Will You please tell me some ways in which I can become even closer to You?

Please WRITE the question as there is MAGIC when you SWITCH to the non-dominant hand. Space to write the question below - or use a separate sheet.

_____

_____

_____

_____

_____

_____

_____

Now, SWITCH the pen to your non-dominant hand. Be patient. Write down the first words that come to you. Let this be easy. Do not stress.
Mother Azna reponds:

_____

_____

_____

_____

_____

_____

_____

_____

QUOTE:

When one door closes, another opens.
But we often look so long and
so regretfully upon the closed door,
that we do not see the one
which has opened for us.

— Alexander Graham Bell

Chapter Eleven

HOW TO MOVE FORWARD

Rebecca: Dear Azna: Thank you for all of the blessings which we are enjoying. The world needs your calming and nurturing. The world is ready to appreciate your ability to move Heaven and Earth.

Mother Azna replies: Darling children, this time of turmoil has, indeed, been a stepping stone for many. Yes, now is the time to choose to step forward and into greater trust and, thus, greater evolution. This is a time of great testing.

Fear not… for naught can touch you, if you stand fast and hold to your faith. I refer to a scripture verse:

When Peter, the Apostle, saw Jesus walking on water, Jesus beckoned for Peter to come and walk on the water with him. As long as Peter kept his eyes on the prize, he walked on top of the water, just as

Jesus was doing. It was only when he took his eyes off of that great Light, that he started to sink.

(Full story can be found at Matthew 14:22-33)

So it is now - in this time of trouble. Keep your eyes steadfast on the Light within. Call upon your Angels, Guides and Light Beings for assistance.

Know this: You are not here by accident. You chose to go through all that you are going through. You always have the power to choose again.

Choose now to only focus on those things that are good. Focus on those things that bring you joy. Release any shame you may feel at seeking joy amidst the suffering of others.

As you fill up your own cup with joy, it spills over to others. For you, simply being a beacon of Light and comfort to your community, could be the reason you opted to incarnate at this time.

Optional Exercise: (Use the instructions at the beginning of this book on Channeling guidance from Mother Azna.)

WRITE with your dominant hand: Dear Mother Azna: Will you please tell me some ways to feel more joy in my life?

Please WRITE the question as there is MAGIC when you SWITCH to the non-dominant hand.
Space to write the question below - or use a separate sheet.

_____

_____

_____

Now, SWITCH the pen to your non-dominant hand. Be patient. Write down the first words that come to you. Let this be easy. Do not stress.
Mother Azna reponds:

_____

_____

_____

_____

_____

_____

_____

_____

Optional UPGRADE Exercise:
(Use the instructions at the beginning of this book on Channeling guidance from Mother Azna.)

WRITE with your dominant hand: Dear Mother Azna: Is there anything that I am doing that is BLOCKING more joy in my life?

Please WRITE the question as there is MAGIC when you SWITCH to the non-dominant hand. Space to write the question below - or use a separate sheet.

_____

_____

_____

Now, SWITCH the pen to your non-dominant hand. Be patient. Write down the first words that come to you. Let this be easy. Do not stress.
Mother Azna reponds:

_____

_____

_____

_____

_____

_____

_____

QUOTE:

I believe that everything happens for a reason. People change so that you can learn to let go. Things go wrong so that you appreciate them when they're right. You believe lies so you eventually learn to trust no one but yourself. And sometimes good things fall apart so better things can fall together.

— Marilyn Monroe

Chapter Twelve

PRAYER TO MOTHER AZNA FOR HELP

Prayer For When You Feel "Broken" Inside:

Rebecca: I give you this prayer to assist you in calling in more power, when you feel that you have failed:

Dear Divine Mother: I feel broken inside. I know my eyes should not be on all of the circumstances around me. I can't seem to help myself. I feel so deeply concerned for all who are in turmoil, including myself. Please help me, Dear Mother.

I ask that You send in Your own League of Angelic Beings - the Thrones - to assist me. Please help me to awaken to my own Divinity within. Fill me with Holy Spirit Light and strength now. Thank you. Amen.

QUOTE:

Your vision will become clear only when you can look into your own heart. Who looks outside, dreams; who looks inside, awakes.

— Carl Jung

Chapter Thirteen

QUIET MINDS FIND SOLUTIONS

Rebecca: Dear Azna: What shall we speak of today?

Mother Azna replies: Let us speak of surrendering to the Divine. By this, I am including the Divine Being that you are - as well as the Divine Beings who help you to be of service.

We are all in service to humanity. By surrendering to your part in this, a great leap forward can be easy. When you have a problem, We see you searching desperately in your mind for a solution.

Your brain waves accelerate faster and faster... until you are in a panic. No good solution is ever forthcoming when you're in panic mode. When a problem assails you... slow down. At that point, it is good to go into a meditative state.

In meditation, your brain waves slow to the perfect rate so that you are able to receive the guidance needed to solve the problem.

Yes, I know that many situations have multiple layers. As you look at the whole of the problem, all kinds of emotions may arise, sending you back into panic mode.

Resist beating yourself up over this. Return to the quietness of your mind and heart. Breathe deeply and calm yourself. Connect your heart to your mind. Realize that you are a Divine Light Being, as you undergo these human experiences.

As you find your place of calm, this is the most advantageous place to ask for My assistance. My intervention is always done in love - Love for you and love for all other parties, yes… even those whom you feel have done you wrong.

You see, darling child, I love ALL of my children, even the naughty ones. You cannot ask me to do anything against any of my children. Yes, you may ask me to place a filter around them to prevent them from harming you.

It will be a filter of Love to help them to see into their own heart. Often a huge problem which you have, is the result of a Soul agreement both parties have in place. Make your request, and then surrender it to Me.

Allow me to do the work. As long as you keep worrying about it, you keep picking the burden back up. That keeps Me from doing My best work on your behalf. You are interfering in the swift solution to your problem.

Not surrendering just means… the solution will take longer.

Here's a prayer to assist you:

Dear Mother Azna: I surrender this problem of, _____, to You. I ask You to address this in the best manner, for the highest good of all, with harm to none. I ask for peace now to settle within my heart. Thank you. Amen.

Azna continues: Now - pay attention. If you want to pick up the worry again, simply forgive yourself and surrender it to Me again. No matter how many times it takes… just re-surrender.

QUOTE:

To the mind that is still, the whole universe surrenders.

— **Lao Tzu**

Chapter Fourteen

PEOPLE WILL ALWAYS FIND MOTHER AZNA WHEN THE TIME IS PERFECT

Rebecca: Dear Mother Azna: I'm reminded NOT to sit, judge and label people who are against you, Dear Mother.

Azna replies: Your labeling words give those who are against Me more power to resist. It is up to each individual when, if ever, they embrace the Divine Mother aspect.

Instead of labeling or criticizing others for their beliefs, understand that it is NOT your job to convince others of My presence. Those who are ready will turn to Me at the perfect time. Some may never do so. Please respect the beliefs of others.

Rebecca: Dear Mother Azna: If a person desires to Channel messages from You, is there a best way to begin?

Mother Azna replies: Yes… a very precise way, which I will share:

- Write me a letter. Just pour out your heart to Me. Say anything… and everything… that you desire. No holding back. Do this on day one.

- On day two, do the exercise to receive more Love, which can be found earlier in this book - only this time - specifically ask that you receive more **Divine Mother Love**.

- On day three, ask Me for a message, using your dominant hand. Refer to the instructions for dominant/non-dominant handwriting, which are found in the beginning of this book. Switch the pen to your non-dominant hand and receive My message.

Rebecca: You have already had the opportunity to do this… if you have made use of the "optional exercises" at the end of some chapters. These Channeling steps will take you to another level!

You may ask the question: Azna, should a person do all three steps in one day, if they are eager to connect with You?

Divine Mother's Answer: **Yes, of course! However, it is most important to write that letter to Me.** Writing something down makes it binding. Read it out loud after you have finished. I am listening and the Angels are listening.

It's important to **KNOW** that you are my Divine child and that I am your Heavenly Mother. Let yourself be vulnerable to my Love.

QUOTE:

Great things are happening in your heart. Divine Love is kindling there, and the flames are expanding. You are changing in a very beautiful way. Stay with me.

— Connie Hubner Channeling Divine Mother

Chapter Fifteen

FROM CHAOS TO BLISS

Rebecca: When you find yourself embroiled in a chaotic experience, you DO have the power to shift it for the better. You could choose to BLESS the situation. That alone will cause a shift in the energy. I know that this can feel very hard to do… yet, I KNOW that you have the power to do this.

Here is a prayer to assist you: Dear Mother Azna: I don't understand why I'm in this situation. Still, I choose to bless all as part of my life experience. I may not now see even one benefit, yet I bless this with Grace.

I surrender this situation to You, Dear Mother, for I surely do not know how to handle these circumstances. Please give me Grace. Please give me strength. Please guide me into forgiveness. I trust you. Thank you. Amen.

Optional Exercise: (Use the instructions at the beginning of this book on Channeling guidance from Mother Azna.)

WRITE with your dominant hand: Dear Mother Azna: Please show me ways that I can be contributing to the agony of this situation and how to remedy this within myself?

Please WRITE the question as there is MAGIC when you SWITCH to the non-dominant hand. Space to write the question below - or use a separate sheet.

_____

_____

_____

_____

_____

_____

Now, SWITCH the pen to your non-dominant hand. Be patient. Write down the first words that come to you. Let this be easy. Do not stress.
Mother Azna reponds:

_____

_____

_____

_____

_____

_____

_____

QUOTE:

Peace begins with a smile.

— Mother Teresa

Chapter Sixteen

BEINGS OF LIGHT - EMBRACE YOUR DIVINITY

Divine Mother says: **Tell no lies.** This is a touchy subject - for no one likes to think that they lie. Yet, the greatest lies that I see, are not lies in the way you might think.

No, the greatest lies are those of denial. When you deny that you are a Divine Being, you cannot see all of the glory that you bring. When you cannot see that Divine Beings desire to warm themselves around the fire of your heart flames, you deny that they're here to help you in the capacity as a partnership.

When you deny that you are more than worthy to have a back-and-forth - co-creative relationship with Us - this is the number one **untruth** with which you have been indoctrinated.

Throw off that cloak of unworthiness, as you would discard an old rag. You no longer need to feel "less than." We wish to work with you, yet not from a place of you being subservient. YOU have the power of the spoken word to bless or curse all things.

You may be asking, how can you bless Us? Communicate with Us. Offer Us your heartfelt service… because together, We serve all of humanity.

How can you curse Us? By denying your own power to call upon Us, to merge with Us, to partner with Us.

Here is a prayer of partnership:

Dear Divine Mother and Beings of Light: I open my heart to You. I sit in silence and listen for Your guidance. I am willing to allow You to show me my power, and to awaken even more of the Divine Essence within me. Amen.

QUOTE:

On this path, let the heart be your guide.

— **Rumi**

Chapter Seventeen

FOLLOWING YOUR HEART TO SUCCESS

Rebecca: Dear Mother Azna: Do you have any advice about success for us today?

Mother Azna replies: I wish to speak of success and the various meanings that it has for all who follow their hearts. You see Beloved Heart - true success can only be obtained when one is following the desires of the heart.

Some think of success as reaching a certain financial status, and if that is something that your heart truly desires, then that may define success for you. Yet, in every instance where you are clamoring for financial status, there are underlying reasons that you desire it.

The number one reason that most people desire financial success is for security. Money equals security to many. Yet, if only money is desired, with no heartfelt reason behind it, there is no pleasure in it.

Consider the story of King Midas. Everything he touched, indeed, turned to gold... even his precious daughter. If you are defining success by financial status, I invite you to look deep and acknowledge all of the other reasons you desire it. This will help you to actualize greater financial status much more quickly than saying, "I want more money."

Let's look at another definition of success. I desire to have more Love in my life. This is actually easy to obtain, for here we make good use of the Law of Reciprocity. Not just people... the entire Universe honors the Law of Reciprocity.

If you desire more Love - give more Love, become more Lovable. However, you cannot give more Love successfully if you do not first Love yourself. Ask for My help in rooting out those things inside yourself that you criticize or find unlovable. This action applies to any type of Love that you are seeking.

Many of you do not realize that you have made a Soul agreement with another person who is very unlovable. This person may feel like a great stumbling block in your path to self-Love, and attracting the Love of others. You may call them enemies. I invite you to view every person in your life as your teacher! You learn SOMETHING from everyone with whom you come into contact.

Even Christ said, "Love your enemies."

This can be very hard to do when this person is like a thorn in your side. Remember this: All Souls Love each other... all personalities do not. **Remember that your enemy is also My child.**

Here is a prayer to help you to transform hatred, disgust, and loathing into, well, at least tolerance:

Dear Azna: I find it impossible to feel any Love at all for: [fill in the blank]. I feel that they have wronged me. Please help me to see the inner child within them... the wounded heart that YOU see.

Please help me to resolve my emotional entanglements. Forgive me when I fail. I surrender these feelings to You. I may have to keep re-surrendering. This person is a great teacher for me.

I release my resentments to You. I release my sense of betrayal to You. I release my struggles with this to You. I, further, release **myself** from all bondage due to this person, event, or situation. Thank You. Amen.

QUOTE:

Worry is a thin stream of fear trickling through the mind. If encouraged, it cuts a channel into which all other thoughts are drained.

— Arthur Somers Roche

Chapter Eighteen

MOTHER AZNA HELPS US TO LET GO

Rebecca: Dear Azna: I have noticed that even when my business problems are solved, I still find several things to worry about. Why is that? And will You please help me to release this habit?

Mother Azna replies: Darling children, this has a lot to do with self judgment. It is a human tendency to look at what is wrong, no matter how minor... instead of looking to see the circumstances and things in life that are wonderful. This is a carryover effect from ages ago when your DNA was tampered with.

Long ago certain beings attempted to make you fearful, in order to make humanity into a slave race. A signal was implanted. This signal responds to any kind of stress as a protective measure. Your neuron systems begin to look for, and dwell upon, any kind of problem that they can find.

This is our attempt to right the wrong, even when there is no wrong, or not much that is wrong. The solution is to notice when you are excessively worrying over minor things… and let them go. This will take some practice, for you have allowed this to become a deeply ingrained habit. Partly, this is an effort at self-preservation. Partly, this is an unconscious effort to please authority figures so as not to get into trouble. This is in part most related to ancient DNA tampering.

You are not a member of a slave race. Each one of you is a Sovereign Being.

Here is what you can do when you find yourself worrying excessively over small things:

- Step One: You can decide to let that worry go. You will have to remind yourself to let go, again and again, as this is new for you. Many of you feel that worrying is a sign of caring.
- Step Two: Say a prayer of relief and decide to trust in the highest good.
- Step Three: You can use visualization about worry. See the worry as completely solved with a happy outcome.

Here is a prayer to help you to release worry over small things:

Dear Azna: Please send your Angels to tap me on the shoulder, when I'm worrying over small things. Ask your Angels to comfort me and whisper in my ear, "Let it go, let it go, let it go." I release any DNA disruptors connected to being a slave race. I acknowledge and officially claim my Sovereignty. Thank you. Amen.

QUOTE:

Trust yourself. Create the kind of self that you will be happy to live with all your life. Make the most of yourself by fanning the tiny, inner sparks of possibility into flames of achievement.

— Golda Meir

Chapter Nineteen

CALM ALLOWS US TO RECEIVE

Rebecca: Dear Azna: We talked about how hard it is to release worry over small things. What can we do when there are really big things wrong in our lives? Things like sickness, relationships falling apart, losing a job, being homeless, or having a lot of trouble with our children. What can we do about those kinds of worries?

Mother Azna replies: Peace. Be still. The first step is always to calm yourself. When you are in a state of panic, or extreme stress, the flow of communication between your body, your mind, and your Spirit becomes blocked.

You can do this calming exercise by using deep, slow breathing. This will calm you, so that you can pray more effectively. Once you are calmer, begin your prayers. Imagine that your petitions are going out and away from your life… as brilliant points of Light.

Know this - every prayer is heard. It is not necessary to keep repeating the same prayer over and over. You are always heard. When you are praying - you are in the sending mode. Energy is going out from you. If you keep repeating the same prayer, it is as if you are not trusting that We hear you. The best remedy for this is to switch into thankfulness mode. This puts you in a position to receive… Yes - to receive answers, to receive guidance, to receive blessings, solutions, and peace.

Here is an example of a mother's prayer for her child. In this case, the child needs healing for an illness.

Dear Mother Azna: My child is sick and in need of healing. Please have mercy on me and this child. Thank You for hearing my plea.

Thank You for Your guidance on what I need to do. Thank You for providing Wisdom to the medical community to inspire correct action. Thank You for sending the perfect help and solutions. I trust that all will be done in Divine Order, and for the highest good of all. Amen.

QUOTE:

You are not an option, a choice or a soft place to land after a long battle. You were meant to be the one.

If you can wrap yourself around the idea that you are something incredible, then you will stop excusing behavior that rapes your very soul.

You were never meant to teach someone to love you. You were meant to be loved.

— **Shannon L. Alder**

Chapter Twenty

YOU MUST TAKE CARE OF YOUR OWN NEEDS FIRST - BEFORE THOSE OF OTHERS

Rebecca: Dear Azna: There is a sense of loneliness and loss in my energy field today. Will You please help me with that?

Mother Azna replies: Yes, Rebecca, take care of your blood sugar first. Eat something and you will find calm.

(I was in distress because my blood sugar was very low. Mother Azna knew this. She asked me to eat something, and then to come back for guidance - so that I would, then, be able to hear and act on it.)

Mother Azna now replies: Putting everyone else's needs before your own... does not serve you. When you sat down to channel Me - before you had any breakfast - you simply were not in the best place to receive guidance.

This was because your blood sugar was low at the time. Other days when you channel before breakfast, it's okay. Your blood sugar is usually fairly well-balanced. The lesson here is simple: **Pay attention to your body's needs.**

Your physical body is your dwelling place. The energy of your physical body either enables or disables psychic communications. When your blood sugar is balanced, you're able to pay better, more focused, attention to the information from Spirit. When any part of your physical being is out of balance, it is slightly more difficult, and sometimes, a **lot more difficult.**

This balancing refers to your chakra systems as well. It is good to begin every channeling session with a quick chakra balance. The most simple way is to touch each chakra and give the command to balance. This is practical information.

To receive guidance more clearly, go into a state of balance as much as possible. You could look at this the same way as foreplay before sex. Sure, you can just hop right into the sex act, yet, without foreplay, there is not as much pleasure, there is no intimacy. Give yourself a few moments for the foreplay of balance, and you will find much more pleasure and intimacy with all Beings of Light.

 Love, Azna.

P.S. from Rebecca: That morning, after I had a bite to eat, and balanced my Chakras… everything in my world felt brighter.

QUOTE:

The greatest gift you can ever give another person is your own happiness.

— Esther Hicks

Chapter Twenty-one

PRAYER TO RECOGNIZE YOUR GIFTS

Rebecca: Here is a prayer to help you to see and realize your own gifts and talents:

Dear Mother Azna: Please help me to see my own talents, and to recognize the help that I am able to give. Please send your Angels to minister to my Spirit - to lift me up so that I may rediscover my joy. As I am lifted up, I share that joy with others. Thank you. Amen.

QUOTE:

There is nothing outside of yourself. Look within. Everything you want is there.

— Rumi

Chapter Twenty-two

CONNECTEDNESS OVERCOMES LONELINESS

Rebecca: Dear Azna: There is much loneliness in the world today. Will You please give us some advice to help us to feel more connected?

Mother Azna replies: Yes, we understand that every person goes through a period of feeling lonely from time to time. This is a good time for selfless listening. Before you rush to find a remedy for your lonely condition… look within. There are changes that you can make within yourself, that help you to get connected more deeply to your heart's desire.

Great evolutionary shifts often happen when people can embrace a time of being alone. It is not necessary to stay in a place where they are feeling lonely. It is advisable to take being alone for a bit - as a good dose of spiritual medicine. Being alone is a perfect time to allow your imagination to run wild and free. Yes, this is a great time to reinvent yourself. Much like a sluggish-seeming caterpillar spends time in the chrysalis, dreaming of flying… so shall it be with you.

QUOTE:

The loneliness you feel is actually an opportunity to reconnect with others and yourself.

— Maxime Lagacé

Chapter Twenty-three

MORE WAYS TO HEAL LONELINESS

Rebecca: Mother Azna: We spoke of people who feel lonely when they are all by themselves. What if one feels lonely even though surrounded by other people?

Mother Azna replies: There is a difference. When one feels lonely or alone, even with people all around - their soul is crying. Yes - crying for sadness to be released. When you feel all alone or lonely in this case, sit and be still. Ask yourself the following questions:

- Question One: Dear Soul: What are you lonely for?
- Question Two: Dear Soul: What kind of energy would help you to feel better?
- Question Three: Dear Soul: Who is trusted to give you that kind of energy?

(For a free video of this exercise: Visit rebeccamarina.com/resources)

After you have done your inner work and desire to have more companionship in your life - here are some things that you can do:

- BE the friend that you, yourself, would like to have.
- Practice listening.
- Send Love out to perfect strangers.
- Smile often.
- Give sincere compliments to others.

There is something complementary that you can sincerely say to almost everyone…

Examples:

Notice that they have nice eyes - **say so**.

Notice that the color they are wearing looks good on them - **say so**.

Notice that they have a nice smile - **say so**.

The world would be a happier place if we all made it a habit to look for the good in others - **and say so!**

Refrain from dwelling on your lack of friends.

Refrain from being argumentative. Let others have their own opinions even if YOU believe otherwise.

Think of ways to make others feel good, let them talk about themselves…. which is everyone's favorite topic.

Pray and ask for like-minded friends.

QUOTE:

Whether you try too hard to fit in or you try too hard to stand out, it is of equal consequence: you exhaust your significance.

— Criss Jami, Healology

Chapter Twenty-four

MOTHER AZNA ON EXHAUSTION

Rebecca: Dear Mother Azna: Please give us some advice about physical exhaustion. I know that this condition affects all of us at some time in our lives.

Mother Azna replies: Perhaps you're not aware of the connection between physical and emotional exhaustion. When you are physically exhausted, yet proud of a job well done, you recover from it very quickly.

What We in the Spirit world are seeing as far more widespread and debilitating, is exhaustion in the emotional and Spiritual realm. When you are exhausted both emotionally and Spiritually, any physical effort seems more difficult.

If you have been feeling very exhausted lately, it is good to examine your heart and emotions for the real source of your exhaustion. There is relief to be found, merely by acknowledging the kind of exhaustion that you have. Acknowledging this, brings it up to the Light for healing.

Here is an example of the way your emotional state can influence your physical state:

Imagine that you have been working very hard all day long. Say that you're packing boxes because you are preparing to move. In addition, you are feeling sad because you don't really want to move to another location. Suddenly your phone rings. You are told that an unknown, but very wealthy benefactor, has just gifted you with a completely free, beautiful home, in the very place that you have always wanted to live.

Not only that... but this person has paid the property taxes twenty-five years in advance. This rich benefactor is even sending movers to finish the packing for you, and taking care of everything.

Do you think your emotional, physical and Spiritual energy would shift? Yes, of course! Instantly you would be revived, as if you had not done a bit of work. This is the power of our emotions over our physical body. The good news is that you don't have to wait for a rich benefactor to present you with a fabulous gift. You can start now.

The next time that you are feeling physically exhausted - you have two choices:

- Choice Number One: Acknowledge the exhaustion, and give yourself time to rest. Do this if you feel that it is best for you.
- Choice Number Two: Acknowledge that there are emotional components to your exhaustion, and bring those components up to the Light.

Here is a prayer to assist you: Dear Mother Azna: I am exhausted in every way. Please send your Angels of strength, comfort and motivation to help me. Thank you. Amen.

Relax and imagine that you are in an Angelic spa. You are experiencing being nourished on every level. Your physical body is nourished. Your mental body is revived. Your Spirit becomes inspired.

Know that you are worthy to have Angels minister to you! You only need to rest for a few minutes, while the Angelic treatments take effect. Then, you will emerge completely refreshed... acting **as if** you are once again full of enthusiasm for life.

QUOTE:

The intuitive mind is a sacred gift and the rational mind is a faithful servant. We have created a society that honors the servant and has forgotten the gift.

— Albert Einstein

Chapter Twenty-five

MOTHER AZNA ON THE THIRD EYE/PINEAL GLAND

Rebecca: Dear Mother Azna: Many people are concerned with opening/activating their Third Eye. Will you please give us some advice on that?

Mother Azna replies: Yes, people desire to work on opening/activating their Third Eye, because they think it will give them super intuition or even magical powers. This is the backwards route. Focus on increasing your intuition. Pray for the needed Wisdom to use it. Intuition without Wisdom is useless as far as Spiritual evolution goes. Pray for Wisdom along with Discernment.

Let's go back to the Third Eye. There is no magical formula for getting it to open or to be activated. There is however, a magical formula to increase your intuition.

How?

You already know that the Pineal gland is the seat of intuition. Some have likened the Pineal to the Ark of the Covenant, a transmitter for talking to God. The Pineal is able to both receive and transmit messages.

The Pineal craves Light - the full-spectrum Light that can only be found in the Divine Feminine realm of Light. As you learn to use My Heart Point Technique method to bring in the full spectrum of Divine Feminine Light, you will find that your intuition increases exponentially.

Question: Why is this so?

Answer: This is so because the Divine Feminine spectrum has a built-in safety feature - Divine Mother Wisdom. Yes, you are bringing in Divine Mother Wisdom as well.

QUOTE:

Gratitude unlocks the fullness of life. It turns what we have into enough, and more. It turns denial into acceptance, chaos to order, confusion to clarity. It can turn a meal into a feast, a house into a home, a stranger into a friend.

— Melody Beattie

Chapter Twenty-six

GRATITUDE IS THE ATTITUDE

Rebecca: Dear Azna: Thank you for all of the good things in my life. Thank you for sending me help when it is needed. Thank you for knowing my heart's desire. Thank you for peace. Thank you for shelter and sustenance.

Mother Azna replies: Dear ones, it is exactly this kind of gratitude energy that attracts even more good things to you. Start out being grateful for even the smallest thing. When your energy gets focused on the good which you already have - it paves the way for even more good to come to you.

This is the most simple and effective way to attract more good into your life that exists.

Do you want more Love in your life?

Be grateful for even the smallest amount of Love that you already have.

Express your gratitude, every way that you can. Put it in writing. Say it out loud. Make it extra powerful by singing it. When you sing, even if you don't sing well, it gets the attention of many, many Beings of Light. It creates a warm fire. They Love to bathe in your fire of joy. Shall we experiment?

Money - I'm very grateful for all of the money that I have. I sing the praises of my money.

Love - I'm very grateful for all of the people who Love me. I sing the praises of Love.

Health - I'm very grateful for the good health that I have. (Come on, you do have some good health.) I sing the praises of my good health.

You will notice that more and more of the things that you write about, and sing about, are coming to you. It is important not to reject any of it, because it may not be the exact match of what you desire.

Keep praising! Keep singing! Keep the faith!

QUOTE:

No problem can be solved from the same consciousness that created it.

— Albert Einstein

Chapter Twenty-seven

BE STILL AND KNOW

Rebecca: Dear Azna: There is a lot of upheaval in the world. Financial systems are crumbling. People are losing their jobs. How can we calm our anxiety, and feel safe in this environment?

Mother Azna replies: There have always been forms of chaos, and even horror, going on somewhere in the world. This is why Jesus said, "The poor will always be with you." This is referenced several times in the New Testament, and even in the Old Testament.

When you see chaos in the world, and feel guided to do something about it - pray for insight. Then spring into action on the guidance which you receive.

It does absolutely no good to sit around and commiserate over the sad state of the world.

In all things - pray for guidance.

Sometimes the guidance could be for you to become very still, and allow Spirits to minister to you. Yes, to minister to your very own upsetting emotions.

Sometimes the guidance could be to take a specific action.

Rebecca: Mother Azna: What can we do if the chaos has affected us directly. For example, we have lost our source of income. Now we cannot pay our bills, buy food, or buy any of those things which we need for survival.

Mother Azna replies: The answer is similar. You are not alone. You have every assistance in the Spiritual realm, yet you may still find yourself in a state of panic.

It's hard to even ask for the assistance that you need - when your emotions are so chaotic that you are blocking any guidance that we are attempting to provide.

(See Helpful Anxiety Releasing Video at Rebeccamarina.com/resources)

Here is a prayer to help you:

Mother Azna: I am frightened for my survival… and for that of my loved ones. Please comfort me. Please send me help and guidance - quickly. Please show me what my action part is in all of this. Thank you. Amen.

You see - we are all partners in the same Divine journey. You are never alone. There is a solution to every problem. When your brainwave activity is going crazy in panic mode - you cannot solve anything.

When you are relaxed and calm - answers come easily to you. This is why having a period of quiet time each day is vitally important, even when you don't have any big problems. Quieting the mind is food for the soul. Remember that you chose this lifetime to evolve. Be still and know.

QUOTE:

When you learn to give yourself a break and feel okay about not being able to live up to impossible standards, then you can begin to get the worry-free rest your mind and body so badly need.

— **Suman Rai**

Chapter Twenty-eight

THE DIVINE ENERGY "LOTTERY"

Rebecca: (The day before Christmas, a few years back)... Dear Azna: This is the holiday season. I feel slow and sleepy. I don't feel like doing much. I feel no sense of urgency to do anything. When I go out, I see the cars bumper to bumper - yet, I feel as if I'm looking at it through my own slow-moving bubble.

Is there something wrong with me?

Should I energize myself, and go jump into the holiday frenzy like many others?

Mother Azna replies: Dear one, we see your energy as a calming influence on others - even if they are not aware of it. Because you are being calm - you energetically influence people around you.

You may not know this, but there are many Light Workers, who are holding quiet space for others. This prevents the busy chaos from getting even more out-of-hand.

Now, there are some souls who hold the quiet space all the time. These wonderful souls are doing all of you a great favor. Occasionally, more quiet souls are needed. This is when the "Lottery" goes into effect.

At this time… you have been chosen. You are not normally a sleepy, quiet person. You are feeling the overwhelming need to rest more, to be quiet more often. Know that you are doing much good in this way.

Your little corner of the world needs more peacefulness, more stability. You are providing that. Of course, you volunteered to have your name put into the Spiritual "Lottery" system - not just for holding space. There are many times that you are called upon to create a certain kind of much-needed energy.

Think of times when you felt compelled to behave in uncharacteristic ways. It is very possible that your

Spirit was being called on to provide a certain boost of energy to just one soul, or to a whole group.

You, yourself, have been the recipient of donated energy many times.

The secret is to honor how you are feeling, whether it be shouting from the rooftops, or spending extra time in bed. When it's Spirit-led - your heart feels really good. It is wise to follow your guidance.

QUOTE:

We should give to others what we intend to get. What enters into a circle will complete a full cycle and return to its origin in kind.

— Hendrith Vanlon Smith, Jr.

Chapter Twenty-nine

MOTHER AZNA ON THE UNIVERSAL LAW OF RECIPROCITY

Rebecca: Dear Azna: What wonderful words do you have for us today?

Azna responds: Let's talk of Reciprocity. This is not what you are accustomed to thinking about when you hear this - for when you hear the word reciprocity, you think of some type of sales pitch, yes?

We feel that if we do a favor for someone, or give a gift to someone, that they will be obligated to do something for you in return.

Don't you realize, dear ones, that it is not necessary to try to activate this law? The Laws of the Universe are always in place - whether you try to activate them or not.

Let's go back to that Law of Reciprocity.

It's working even now - without you having to do anything to activate it.

You breathe out carbon dioxide. Plants take it in, and give you back oxygen.

The Law of Reciprocity can work as a positive force - or it can work as a negative force. But it is always at work.

For example...When you pour pollutants into water, you receive back the negative effects of this action - polluted water.

Whatever you do... is returned to you in kind, but not necessarily at the moment that you do it. Yet, sooner or later, the Law of Reciprocity serves all.

Refrain from placing so much focus on the actions of others - and imagining what THEIR reciprocity could be!

Pay attention to your own heart's guidance.

You are responsible only for your own soul's journey.

Yet, you may be guided to be a shepherd, a guide, a protector - or even a savior to others.

Still, each person is responsible **ONLY** for their own journey.

Now, let us speak of the other half of the Law of Reciprocity - the receiving back part.

Many Lightworkers are constantly saying NO to receiving - because they do not approve of the source. Or they do not feel that they deserve to receive anything.

PAY ATTENTION - this is very important: To say a prayer requesting blessings - then trying to dictate where those blessings come from - is not helping your evolution.

Remember that the Law of Reciprocity is always working.

It is only when you refuse a thing that you put a kink in the works. **Be willing to receive everything**. Bless it and receive it - no matter where it comes from. **Even those who sometimes perpetuate evil can be moved by Spirit to do good at times.**

Everything is relative to one's point of view.

One type of religion often looks down on another type of religion. Yet almost all religions have programs to help the poor and needy.

Mother Teresa was a devout Catholic, yet she never tried to convert anyone. She simply loved and cared for people. She gave many a chance to die in dignity, instead of leaving them to die in the street.

How did Mother Teresa receive Soul Satisfaction?

Mother Teresa received Great Soul Satisfaction. Every person whom she helped, gave another surge of joy to her heart. She cared nothing for fame. She cared deeply for her mission - and for the Sisters who helped her.

Mother Teresa protected her fellow Nuns by making SURE that they all had the opportunity for some quiet time each day. She KNEW that only by going within, could they have the strength to accomplish the tasks which they faced in daily service.

Each of you has your own journey.

Each of you knows what makes your own heart happy.

Each of you can begin to share with others some of your own heart happiness!

The Universe will multiply your sharing back to you - according to your willingness to receive.

From now on - when someone offers you something - take it! Be willing to receive it. Bless it - and bless them! You will see mighty changes in your life.

Love, Azna.

Rebecca: Later that day, I was enjoying some toast and using it to soak up some really good pure maple syrup. So... I inquired: Mother: What about this delicious syrup that I'm enjoying?

I don't see how this is reciprocal for the maple tree. Azna replies: Some things come just to serve, and that is their way of receiving.

Again, place your eyes upon your own journey.

Know this - every being has their own soul purpose to fulfill.

Everything - animate or inanimate - plays a part in the whole.

Look within, to your own heart's longing, and there you will find the answers that YOU need.

Always return back to your own heart.

Be willing to let others have their journey. If you are guided from within to intervene on another's behalf - then do so.

If you continually turn inward to find your own answers, all will be well. Peace be with you and remember... **you can do no wrong in my eyes.**

Your Loving Divine Mother, Azna.

QUOTE:

The secret of life, though, is to fall seven times and to get up eight times.

— **Paulo Coelho, <u>The Alchemist</u>**

Chapter Thirty

ENERGY EXERCISE TO ACTIVATE YOUR THIRD EYE

In order to activate your Third Eye more fully - use dominant/non-dominant handwriting. (Refer to the complete instructions at the beginning of this book.)

Use your dominant hand to WRITE: Dear Pineal Gland: How can I help you to become more activated?

Now, SWITCH the pen, and receive the answer through your non-dominant hand.

Then - SWITCH the pen back to your dominant hand, and WRITE: Dear Azna: How can I develop more Wisdom and Discernment?

Now, SWITCH the pen back to your non-dominant hand, and receive guidance from Mother Azna.

Always think about both sides when you are asking for guidance. Think of yourself - and think of whom this guidance might affect. When you receive guidance that is for another person, it is not always wise to share it with them at that moment.

Pay attention to your Discernment.

If you look back over your life, you will notice that you ALWAYS felt some restriction, or "gut feeling," when something "bad" was about to happen. Many times, you went against your own gut instinct, and made huge mistakes in money, relationships, and even health issues.

Another word for Discernment could be… "gut feelings."

Even secular professionals will warn you to pay close attention to your gut!

If you are about to walk down a very dark street at night, and you feel a warning bell go off in your gut - **pay attention**!

If you are about to make a financial investment and your stomach ties you in knots… **pay attention**!

Especially, when you are in a new relationship, pay attention to those "red flags" that you so easily excuse or "sweep under the rug."

If you receive guidance on Spiritual matters… pay very close attention to the feeling stirring in your stomach before you reveal it to others.

Sometimes, you can be so very excited about some new Spiritual revelation, that you desire to share it with everyone!

Beware and pay attention… Not everyone is ready to receive what you have. Trust the Divine that ALL will receive what they need, at the perfect time for them.

In summary… "Gut instinct" is very closely related to Discernment.

No matter what name you give it, this is your chance to pay attention, and **TRUST** your own intuition.

QUOTE:

Worrying is carrying tomorrow's load with today's strength - carrying two days at once.
It is moving into tomorrow ahead of time.
Worrying doesn't empty tomorrow of its sorrow, it empties today of its strength.

— Corrie Ten Boom

Chapter Thirty-one

MOTHER AZNA ON THE 2020 WINTER SOLSTICE/ASTROLOGICAL GREAT CONJUNCTION

On December 21, 2020, the world experienced a rare Astrological occurrence. The Winter Solstice and The Great Conjunction were paired together in a formation that had not occurred at the same time for 800 years!

Rebecca had a conversation with Mother Azna to gain insight for all of us on the benefits of this powerful event…

Dear Mother Azna: Do you have any insights for us… looking back on that most auspicious day?

Mother Azna responded: Lift your hearts and be glad - for that was a new beginning for all of humanity. New sources of Prime Creator's Benevolent Light are still being poured out upon all of Creation.

That was a time of choosing a new and higher path.
You can allow your thoughts to take you there!

Take a cue from the Holy Christian scriptures:

Finally my brothers and sisters, whatever is true, whatever is noble, whatever is right, whatever is pure, whatever is lovely, whatever is admirable - if anything is excellent or praiseworthy - think about these things! Philippians 4:8

This is still a special time to let your Light shine. Be a help to your brothers and sisters today by saying: Please show me how I may serve.

It may be that your best aspect of service today is to get quiet within your own heart.
What does your heart need to feel nurtured?
It is only when you go within, that you find your true path to service.

On this day - and every day - find the time to nurture your own soul before jumping up to serve others.

Choose Light this day… and every day.
Choose to think thoughts of your heart's desires.
So many times have I spoken of honoring your heart's desires, as those very desires are the reason you came forth into this Incarnation.

Make every day a New Beginning.
Forgive the past.
Forgive your past mistakes.
Forgive the mistakes of others.

Be Born Anew!
Choose to be Born Anew every day!

Choose every day your highest path - by taking time to commune with your heart and your own Divinity. Even when you feel overwhelmed by all that life can toss your way… Choose the Light.

Your heart knows the Highest Path. The path of Light will NEVER lead you astray!

Do not place your attention on the path of others.
YOUR OWN PATH is the ONLY ONE for which you are RESPONSIBLE.

In your quest to be of service to mankind, take care of your own heart's needs first.
When you give from a place of contentment, your gift is so much more valuable.
The gate is now open! The vast flow of new, higher energies has been released.

This flow will not cease.
You have a choice to bathe in these new energies of Light – or not.

This is still a time of seeking the higher Light by going within more deeply.
The more time that you take to be still and acknowledge that you are **worthy** to receive more Light, more Gifts, more Love – the more you will **have**... **so** the more you will be **able** to **share**.

When your cup is filled with the Light of the Divine, it cannot help but spill over, and go where it is most needed.

Love, Mother Azna.

Optional Exercise: (Use the instructions at the beginning of this book on Channeling guidance from Mother Azna.)

WRITE with your dominant hand: Dear Mother Azna: How can I attract more Light and Love into my life?

Please WRITE this question as there is MAGIC when you SWITCH to the non-dominant hand to write your answer.
(Space to write the question below - or use a separate sheet.)

_____

_____

Now, SWITCH the pen to your non-dominant hand. Be patient. Write down the first words that come to you. Let this be easy. Do not stress.
Mother Azna reponds:

_____

_____

_____

_____

QUOTE:

Love is the Divine Mother's arms; when those arms are spread, every Soul falls into them.

— **Hazrat Inayat Khan**

Chapter Thirty-two

FINAL WORDS OF ENCOURAGEMENT

From Divine Mother Azna:

Rest in the assurance that all is well with your Soul. It is when the heart becomes troubled that doubt, fear, and anxiety creep in, and sabotage your efforts.

The biggest source of doubt is your tendency to dwell on what is wrong… instead of what is right.

It is a fact that there is a big "inner critic" running your life in many cases.
When you listen to that ugly voice… it NEVER has anything good to say!

This is how you tell the difference between true guidance… and negative "inner critic" voices.

True guidance does, indeed, come through in that "still small voice" that is spoken of in the Christain scriptures.

As you are tuning into guidance, ask yourself… Is this guidance making me feel good?
Is this guidance encouraging?
Do I feel happiness as I take in this guidance?

It is possible for negative voices to try to creep in under the guise of… "it's for your own good."

Yes, it is true that there may be something in your life that needs to be transformed. Perhaps you have some detrimental habits that are slowing your forward progression.

It is possible that there are others in your life that are like millstones around your neck. Find the courage to have fewer interactions with these people.

Whatever it is that is hindering your happiness or forward progress, will be revealed to you… gently and easily.

Here is a prayer to ask for guidance on more Happiness and Prosperity in your life:

Dear Mother Azna: Please reveal to me those things that are hindering my Happiness, Health or Prosperity. Please do this gently… and in the perfect timing. I desire to be ready to make the needed changes, as easily and painlessly as possible.

Your child, (insert your name),
Thank you.
Amen.

Mother Azna says: I am here for you, no matter how you are feeling.
When you are happy, I share your happiness.
When you are troubled, my Love seeks to comfort you.
Please accept the Love and comfort which I offer you. Call on Me.

Be kind to yourself.
Forgive yourself often.
Be looking for the GOOD in yourself and others.
Yes, put on a pair of rose-colored glasses!

Mother Azna Says: Always Remember This: YOU CAN DO NO WRONG IN MY EYES!

QUOTE:

Every moment is made glorious
by the light of love.

— Rumi

From Rebecca:
Please visit Rebeccamarina.com/resources
for beautiful guided meditations that will uplift and inspire you.

To learn more about a session with a Heart Point Technique Master.
(HPT is a healing modality from Divine Mother - demonstrated in this book)
Visit: https://rebeccamarina.com/hpt/hpt-masters/

To obtain details for private sessions with Rebecca - email her at:
Rebecca@rebeccamarina.com
Please put "sessions" in the subject line.

www.ingramcontent.com/pod-product-compliance
Lightning Source LLC
Chambersburg PA
CBHW040241130526
44590CB00049B/4089